GREAT

STORE DESIGN

2

Winners from the
Institute of Store Planners/Visual
Merchandising and Store Design
Annual Competition

D1486096

ROCKPORT
PUBLISHERS

Rockport Publishers • Rockport, Massachusetts

First published in the United States of America by:
Rockport Publishers, Inc.
146 Granite Street
Rockport, Massachusetts 01966-1299
Telephone: (508) 546-9590
Fax: (508) 546-7141

Distributed to the book trade and art trade in the United States by:
North Light, an imprint of
F & W Publications
1507 Dana Avenue
Cincinnati, Ohio 45207
Telephone: (800) 289-0963

Other Distribution by:
Rockport Publishers
Rockport, Massachusetts 01966-1299

ISBN 1-56496-301-2

10 9 8 7 6 5 4 3 2 1

VM+SD/ST Publications Production Editor: **Diane Borton**
Designer: **Sara Day Graphic Design**
Cover Photograph: **Doug Landreth** (*store featured on page 55*)
Back Cover Photographs: **(top to bottom) Douglas Dun page 7, Mark Steele, Fitch Inc. page 31 and Llew Reszka page 71**

Manufactured in China by Regent Publishing Services Limited

GREAT STORE DESIGN

Since its founding nearly one hundred years ago, *Visual Merchandising and Store Design* magazine has reported on all aspects of retail visual marketing with particular emphasis on display, store planning, and design. In *Great Store Design 2*, the editors of *VM+SD* have compiled the most significant store projects of 1995 in cooperation with the Institute of Store Planners. These award-winning projects were determined by a panel of distinguished judges who deliberated over more than 150 submissions. They evaluated the submissions on five aspects of great retail design: store planning, visual merchandising, lighting, graphics, and innovation. The 42 stores you'll find on these pages exemplify the power in those five design components.

Through photographs and floor plans, *Great Store Design 2* presents the most current in retail design. The book is intended to serve as an example of creative excellence in design for visual merchandisers, store planners, designers, and architects. You'll see the period looks of the Arts and Crafts movement and Classical era in details and materials. There are also clean, spare designs in metal and glass, painted and stained concrete, and wood—from beautiful veneers and solids to the uncut, untreated variety. You'll also find the latest in store planning and environmental design in the major categories, from department stores to specialty shops, mass merchandisers and entertainment retail.

The elements of great store design bring influences and trends from around the world and across cultures to create successful shopping environments—ones that suit the merchandise, the community, and, most importantly, the customer.

In assembling the environments and materials of some of the best, *VM+SD* offers a volume from which to draw ideas, innovations, and inspiration, not only for store designers and planners, but for all involved in the beauty and science of selling.

The Editors of VM+SD

TABLE OF CONTENTS

STORE OF THE YEAR

POTTERY BARN

CHESTNUT STREET,
SAN FRANCISCO, CALIFORNIA

DESIGN
BACKEN ARRIGONI & ROSS, INC.
SAN FRANCISCO, CALIFORNIA
RICHARD ALTUNA
LOS ANGELES, CALIFORNIA

Design of this store incorporates an adaptive reuse of an urban building. Located on the site of the 1914 Panama Pacific Exposition, the project's architects at Backen, Arrigoni & Ross recycled the antique joists from the vintage 1950 facade to echo the "classicism" of the Exposition.

The building was gutted and the shell's wood truss ceiling removed, then put back with the addition of rough-sawn cedar plywood. The two-story interior features a soaring pyramidal skylight crowning its center. Decorative light fixtures developed for the store include pendants and wall sconces.

The walls are composed of the existing structure's exposed concrete and a warm taupe Italian plaster. Other natural materials include Western Red Cedar for all fixtures, unstained cedar ceilings and a concrete floor.

The store is divided into three zones: "Grand Lobby," "Table Top Shop," and "Design Studio." Decorative accessories are presented around a fireplace in the Grand Lobby while all home furnishing are grouped in the Design Studio in the rear. Signature displays identifying the three zones are presented on steel "draw bridge shelves" located in niches above. (This store was featured in the October 1995 issue of VM+SD.)

Photography by Douglas Dun, San Francisco

SECTION

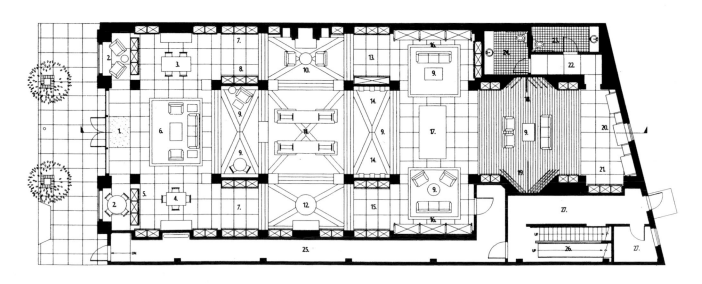

FLOOR PLAN

FIRST PLACE

MARSHALL FIELD'S

NORTHBROOK COURT,
NORTHBROOK, ILLINOIS

DESIGN
THE PAVLIK DESIGN TEAM
FT. LAUDERDALE, FLORIDA

Open design of this newly renovated three-level Marshall Field's visually exposes the entire expanse of each floor. Architecturally, the 275,000-square-foot store features huge rotundas, promenades, and cruciform shopping spaces. Proscenium arches create entrances to the various apparel and home fashions departments.

Flooring consists of light marble aisles inset with contrasting accents. Wall systems and fixtures are movable for maximum flexibility. Each department features varying color palettes. Light residential woods are used in the fashion accessories department, in contrast to the ebony casework used in the fine home department.

At the heart of the store is a three-story atrium incorporating escalators, elevator and a custom, oversized Marshall Field's signature clock.

Photography by Myro Rosky, Ft. Lauderdale, Florida

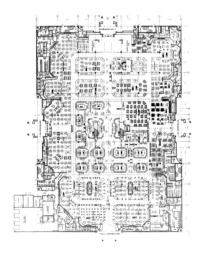

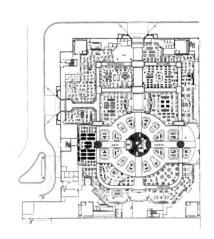

BLOOMINGDALE'S

OLD ORCHARD SHOPPING CENTER,
SKOKIE, ILLINOIS

DESIGN
FRCH DESIGN WORLDWIDE
NEW YORK CITY

Bloomingdale's new 200,000-square-foot store incorporates an open, asymmetrical floor plan with new mobile floor fixtures, greater illumination and a light color palette. In place of a central escalator well, the designers opted to raise ceiling heights to 12 to 15 feet, adding an oculus. Natural light plays a major role in the store. The second-floor women's and the first floor men's departments feature 40-foot-wide banks of windows with mechanized shades designed to filter natural light by day and act as a reflective panel at night.

Interior walls are minimal. Instead, a variety of fixtures at various heights allow for merchandising departments. In men's, for instance, track-mounted sliding panels accept hanging goods. All loose fixtures in the women's and kids' departments are on wheels, allowing for easy reconfiguring.

In addition, Bloomingdale's experimented with special fixturing to allow both open and assisted selling. In home fashions, "sliver shops"—long, open showcases—are positioned in the middle of aisles. The jewelry department features two-sided freestanding showcases accessible from all sides to encourage shoppers to view the merchandise from all sides.

Photography by Peter Paige, Harrington Park, New Jersey

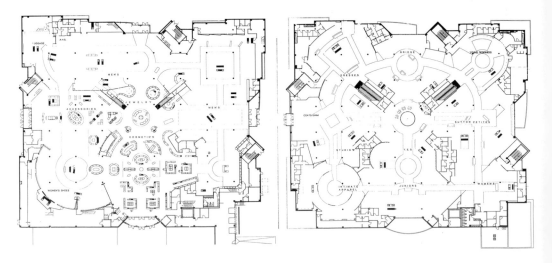

BURDINES

BRANDON TOWN CENTER,
BRANDON, FLORIDA

DESIGN
THE PAVLIK DESIGN TEAM
FT. LAUDERDALE, FLORIDA

Designed to enhance its "Florida store" image, this new 140,000-square-foot Burdines features an open floor plan with split escalators that allows customers a direct view through the entire store. Architecturally, the store recalls its native state through illuminated palm tree columns throughout the space and sand colored ceramic tile for main aisles.

The pastel palette includes turquoise, seafoam green, shell whites and flamingo pink. Fixturing ranges from light wood tables to pink upholstered settees. Natural light is provided from the central oculus and cove lights.

Photography by Myro Rosky, Ft. Lauderdale, Florida

NEW OR TOTALLY RENOVATED
SHOP WITHIN A DEPARTMENT
STORE FOR APPAREL
AND/OR ACCESSORIES, OR HOME
FASHIONS AND HOUSEWARES

FIRST PLACE

MICROSOFT

NEBRASKA FURNITURE MART,
OMAHA, NEBRASKA

DESIGN
RETAIL PLANNING ASSOCIATES, L.P.
COLUMBUS, OHIO

Designed to encourage curiosity and
interactivity, this new shop simplifies
software shopping by offering access to
Microsoft's full product line and its features. Ceiling-suspended curved graphic
panels define department boundaries,
while mobilized light wood and stainless
steel fixtures allow easy configuration
and product mixing. Interactive kiosks
are integrated into the merchandising
system.

Photography by Jerry Wisler, Dayton, Ohio

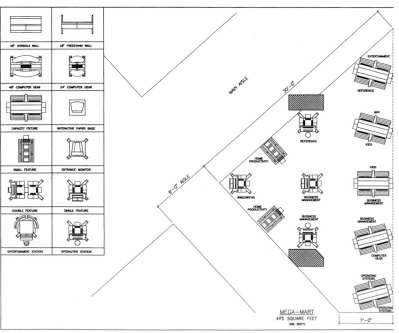

NEW OR TOTALLY RENOVATED
SHOP WITHIN A DEPARTMENT
STORE FOR APPAREL
AND/OR ACCESSORIES, OR HOME
FASHIONS AND HOUSEWARES

HONORABLE MENTION

NIKE SHOP

AT MARSHALL FIELD'S, STATE STREET,
CHICAGO, ILLINOIS

DESIGN
NIKE INC.
BEAVERTON, OREGON

A floor-to-ceiling glass wall offers easy visibility of the products, brand and athletic presentation within this small, but open space. The curved footwear wall houses the full range of Nike products, all under the three-dimensional, familiar "Swoosh" logo. Easy-to-move, utility seating is dispersed throughout. "Concept boxes," standing over seven feet tall, provide variable shelving and panel configurations with additional storage in back. Each fixture accepts footwear, apparel, and accessories.

Photography by Hedrich Blessing, Chicago

JUST DO IT.

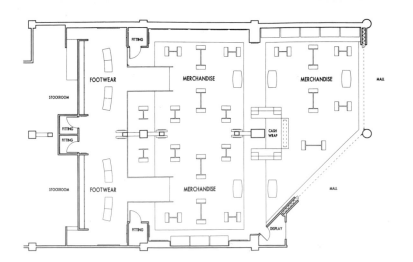

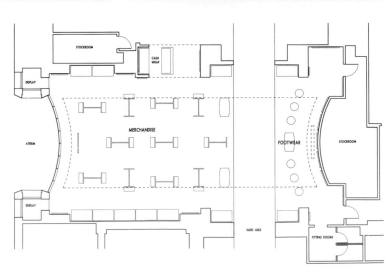

NEW OR TOTALLY RENOVATED
SHOP WITHIN A DEPARTMENT
STORE FOR APPAREL
AND/OR ACCESSORIES, OR HOME
FASHIONS AND HOUSEWARES

HONORABLE MENTION

1. C. B.
BLOOMINGDALE'S

THIRD AVENUE, NEW YORK CITY

DESIGN
MATSUYAMA INTERNATIONAL CORP.
NEW YORK CITY

The designers' objective was to create a simple, clear space with minimal characteristics. Fixtures consist of panels—supported by black poles—that "appear to float" between the floor and ceiling. Though simple in design, these flexible units have interchangeable shelves and face-outs. A 360-degree rotating display, located in the shop's center features a graphic panel front backed with shelving. Other merchandisers consist of T-stands and forms with bases inspired by Herman Miller seating. The shop's flooring is artificial stone with steel inlays.

Photography by Paul Warchol Photography, New York City

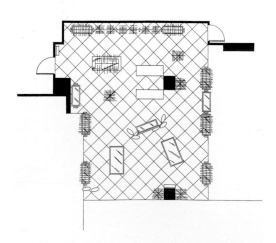

PLANET REEBOK

LINCOLN SQUARE,
NEW YORK CITY

DESIGN
FITCH INC.
WORTHINGTON, OHIO

To draw interest, an interactive window display enables customers to view Planet Reebok athletes and commercials—even when the store is closed. The overall environment utilizes warm, natural materials accented by metals. With a small change in hardware, the modular fixtures can be modified to accept hanging or folded merchandise.

Dividing the men's and women's areas while housing footwear is a curved main aisle. This center aisle is lined with custom showcases which display up to four of the latest shoe styles, accompanied by continuously playing videos. Customers have access to an interactive kiosk located at the center of the store.

Photography by Mark Steele, Fitch Inc.,
Worthington, Ohio

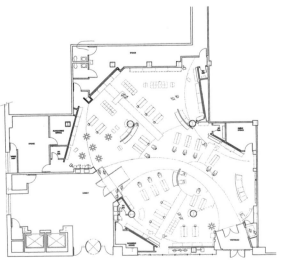

SPECIALTY STORE UNDER 5,000
SQUARE FEET FOR APPAREL
AND/OR ACCESSORIES

HONORABLE MENTION

MONSOON

NATICK MALL,
NATICK, MASSACHUSETTS

DESIGN
BERGMEYER ASSOCIATES, INC.
BOSTON, MASSACHUSETTS

The retailer's emphasis on natural fiber apparel and accessories served to inspire the store design. The space is characterized by fluid lines and high levels of craftsmanship as well as attention to detail. The designers mixed natural materials such as patinaed steel for signage, gold leaf for soffits, and weathered slate for thresholds. A frieze of hand cast and painted medallions punctuate the upper walls. Small-aperture downlights scattered across the ceiling and indirect cove lights are the main source of illumination. A large, sculpted hat "chandelier" is located near the cashwrap and accessory area.

Photography by Lucy Chen Photography, Boston

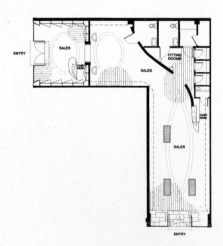

NIKE SHOP

EATON'S CENTER METROTOWN MALL, VANCOUVER

DESIGN
NIKE, INC.
BEAVERTON, OREGON

Its large entrance and prominent logo can be seen far down the mall at Eaton Center. Once inside, customers encounter high-capacity fixtures, with interchangeable shelving and rods, designed to Nike's exacting specifications. As with other Nike spaces, seven-foot-tall "concept boxes" house footwear, apparel and accessories. The Nike sports story and brand identity is seen in the Nike-Air® chairs, Waffle outsole graphic, and the hardwood floors resembling a sports court.

Photography by Hedrich Blessing, Chicago

FIRST PLACE

EDDIE BAUER

POST STREET,
SAN FRANCISCO, CALIFORNIA

DESIGN
FRCH DESIGN WORLDWIDE
CINCINNATI, OHIO

Located in the landmark Gumps' building, the exterior was re-designed to resemble its original Italianate style. Inside, the three-level, 28,600-square-foot store was gutted and restructured. The mezzanine level was removed while a storage area and central atrium with escalators were created. In the escalator well, customers view back-lit graphics of West Coast nature and large iron-detailed chandeliers. Each level echoes the store's use of rich natural materials including wood, metal, and leather. Stones, native to the Northwest, are used for flooring signaling the aisleways.

Photography by Paul Bielenberg, Los Angeles

HONORABLE MENTION

BHS

GRAFTON CENTRE,
CAMBRIDGE, ENGLAND

DESIGN
20/20 DESIGN & STRATEGY CONSULTANTS
LONDON, ENGLAND

Customers are greeted by a two-level, 35-foot-high glass showcase featuring five key departments including mens, womens, childrens, housewares and lingerie. Topped with an American cherry curved canopy, the showcase unites the entrances on both levels.

The designers created merchandise showcases called "epicenters" to guide customers as they enter each department. Each epicenter is designed to reflect the department's personality from etched glass back panels and a translucent fabric canopy in lingerie to a plum-colored proscenium with American cherry lining in men's. Designed to encourage circulation, designers removed walkways throughout the store and incorporated moveable walls to allow mobility within departments.

Photography by Jon O'Brien, London

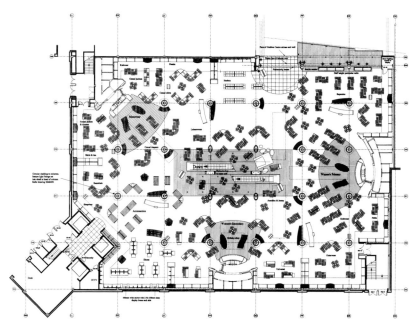

HONORABLE MENTION

THE ORIGINAL
LEVI'S STORE

57TH STREET,
NEW YORK CITY

DESIGN
BERGMEYER ASSOCIATES, INC.
BOSTON, MASSACHUSETTS

For Levi's new flagship location, the designers wanted to create a state-of-the-art, multi-media environment. A stainless steel and granite facade allows maximum exposure of the inside. An atrium unifies the store's four floors with monumental stainless steel stairs and an elevator. Flooring consists of Scandinavian beechwood with inlaid red strips and granite tile walkways. Red slab walls are a trademark reference to Levi's internationally recognized red tab. Eight interactive kiosk directories (available in English, French, German, and Spanish) on the ground level are designed to assist customers' navigation of the store.

Photography by Chun Y Lai Photography,
New York City

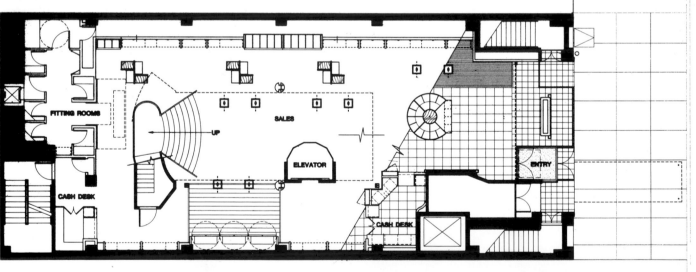
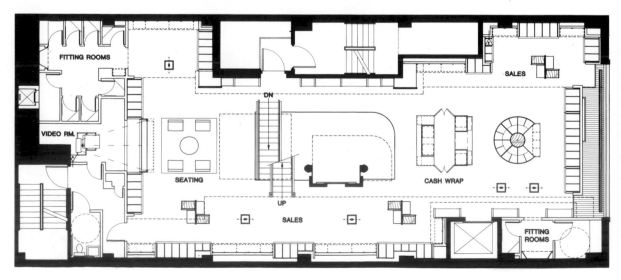

SPECIALTY STORE UNDER 5,000
SQUARE FEET FOR HARD GOODS,
HOUSEWARES, ETC.

NOTE: FIRST PLACE WAS POTTERY BARN
WHICH IS STORE OF THE YEAR

HONORABLE MENTION

GLOBAL NEWS

VANCOUVER INTERNATIONAL AIRPORT
RICHMOND, BRITISH COLOMBIA, CANADA

DESIGN
SUNDERLAND INNERSPACE DESIGN, INC.
VANCOUVER

This 945-square-foot shop is easily identified by an illuminated, blown-glass globe on its facade. The globe is repeated inside on a curved soffit. An inlaid floor creates a world map as it would appear from space in blues and greens. Inlaid terra-cotta strips represent longitudinal lines that meet at the circular, central fixture. Wall-mounted video monitors provide a sense of movement. Lighting is designed to highlight products during the day and evoke images of stars at night.

Photography by Rob Melnychuk Photography, Vancouver

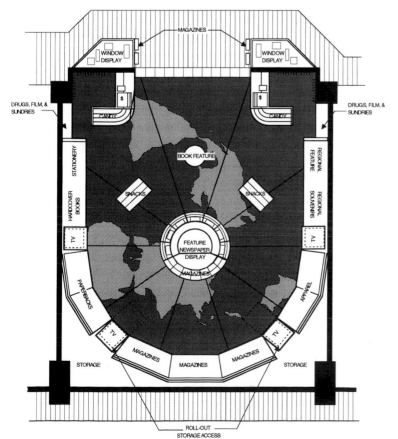

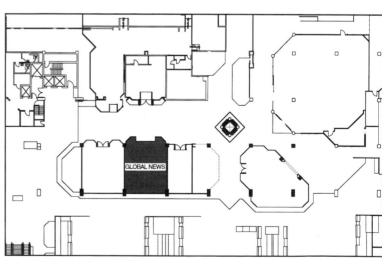

HONORABLE MENTION

EXPLORE MORE STORE

PACIFIC SCIENCE CENTER,
SEATTLE, WASHINGTON

DESIGN
SMASH
SEATTLE, WASHINGTON

Remodeling this 1,700-square-foot gift and educational resource store was challenging due to its mezzanine level location. The space's 18-foot-high ceiling and 8-foot-tall perimeter walls were exploited to make the store visible from below. The new store was approached as an extension of the exhibits with each zone representing a different subject. Standing guard at the center of the store is a "Look-Out Tower" cashwrap overlooking a 30-foot-long shelved wall. Shelving is anchored by seven sculptures on the soffit, each trimmed in natural, recycled elements. A reproduction of a pre-Aztec temple encloses an office while remaining the store's dominant figure.

Photography by Doug Landreth Studios, Seattle

SPECIALTY STORE OVER 5,000
SQUARE FEET FOR HARD GOODS,
HOUSEWARES, ETC.

FIRST PLACE

WILLIAM ASHLEY FINE CHINA

TORONTO

DESIGN
CHRISTOPHER BARRISCALE ARCHITECTS
NEW YORK CITY

The designers opted to create a boutique atmosphere for this 24,000-square-foot store offering fine tabletop items. Warm neutral colors, combined with marble, glass, wood, and carpeting are used in ways to define product departments. A giftware area leads customers into the store's central rotunda housing dinnerware. Fixturing is customized within each department, from tower fixtures of lacewood and stainless steel in the giftware to sycamore and glass "screen" fixtures in the silver area.

Photography by Richard Johnson, Toronto

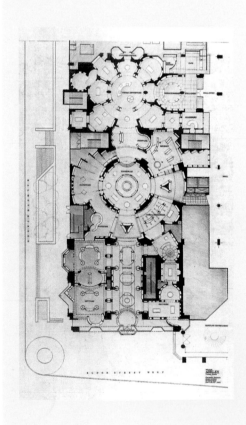

SPECIALTY STORE OVER 5,000
SQUARE FEET FOR HARD GOODS,
HOUSEWARES, ETC.

HONORABLE MENTION

SAM GOODY

HORTON PLAZA,
SAN DIEGO, CALIFORNIA

DESIGN
MUSICLAND GROUP, INC.
MINNETONKA, MINNESOTA

Charged with creating an environment that is both entertaining and educational, the designers created the look and feel of a music stage. Ceiling planes, suspended from the ceiling, are used throughout the store to emphasize product categories. A classical architectural column capitol, with an angel emerging from it, announces the Jazz and Classical section.

Both entrances into this two-level store displays reverse channel signs with exposed neon. Fabric coffee cups, cherubs, and wood toys are suspended in the space adjacent to the split escalators and guide customers to the cafe under central atrium space.

The cafe features end-grain wood flooring differentiating it from colored concrete used elsewhere. Listening stations in the cafe use black granite counters and coated diamond plate steel ramps and stairs.

Photography by Brewster & Brewster Photography, Weldon Brewster, Glendale, California

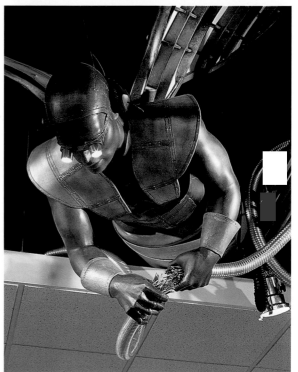

SPECIALTY STORE OVER 5,000
SQUARE FEET FOR HARD GOODS,
HOUSEWARES, ETC.

HONORABLE MENTION

POTTERY BARN

WESTHEIMER BOULEVARD,
HOUSTON, TEXAS

DESIGN
BACKEN ARRIGONI & ROSS INC.
SAN FRANCISCO, CALIFORNIA

As in other Pottery Barn locations, the design utilizes natural materials including antique Southern Yellow Pine for flooring, cedar board for the ceiling, and Italian plaster. An effort was made to incorporate the original structure into the design. In the Grand Lobby, for example, the original concrete structure is exposed at the ceiling.

At the front of the store the Table Top Shop features hutches anchoring each wall with "drawbridge" display shelves above. A 20-by-20-foot skylight highlights the central Grand Lobby area exposing the natural concrete ceiling.

(Other Pottery Barn locations were featured in the October 1995 issue of VM+SD.)

Photography by Douglas Dun, San Francisco

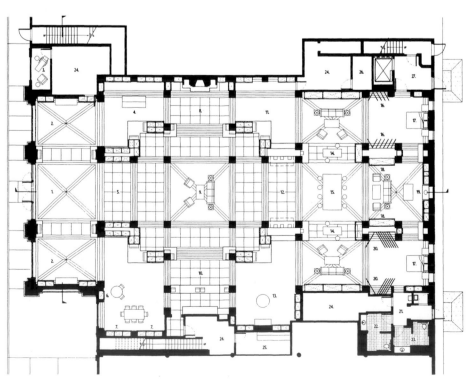

FLOOR PLAN

FIRST PLACE

BRUNO'S SUPERCENTER

SANDY SPRINGS PLACE,
ATLANTA

DESIGN
PROGRAMMED PRODUCTS CORPORATION
PLYMOUTH, MICHIGAN

Design of this "supercenter" features an upscale environment with a strong visual presentation. Awnings and neon were incorporated into signage. Overscaled wall murals focusing on local historical landmarks are featured in dairy and meat departments. New features include custom fixturing, solid surfaces, and accent lighting in the prep and kiosk service areas.

Photography by Llew Reszka, Plymouth, Michigan

HONORABLE MENTION

VIC'S WORLD CLASS MARKET

GRAND RIVER AVENUE,
NOVI, MICHIGAN

DESIGN
PROGRAMMED PRODUCTS CORPORATION
PLYMOUTH, MICHIGAN

In creating a shopping area reminiscent of a small European town square, the designers implemented period signage and materials such as ornamental pressed tin for ceilings and facades, aged copper, actual brick, and faux limestone. The exterior resembles a large farmers' market with its large arched entryway and brightly colored signage. Inside, produce and gourmet groceries located in the center are surrounded by meat, fish, deli and bakery specialty departments.

Photography by Llew Rezka, Plymouth, Michigan

HONORABLE MENTION

LIQUOR CONTROL BOARD OF ONTARIO (LCBO)

QUEEN STREET EAST,
TORONTO

DESIGN
THE INTERNATIONAL DESIGN GROUP
TORONTO

This two-story glass-front exposes the mural, "The Origins Of Alcohol" designed by Antonio Cangemi, over the entryway. Once inside, a suspended ceiling is entwined with wrought-iron vines. Contrasting with the natural beechwood flooring and fixturing are the pewter finished wrought-iron details as seen in floor stripes and wall fixtures. Suspended from the wall and ceiling are arched wrought iron vines with elliptical blade signs featuring the various wine sections. At the back of the store special vintage wines are showcased in cubes.

Photography by Design Archives, Toronto

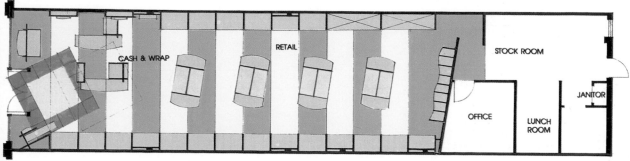

FIRST PLACE

IL FORNAIO

LORTON AVENUE,
BURLINGAME, CALIFORNIA

DESIGN
BACKEN ARRIGONI & ROSS, INC.
SAN FRANCISCO, CALIFORNIA

This project involved the revitalization of three adjacent buildings with the uncovering of the original plaster and masonry details. Inside, the existing structure was exposed to create a dining room featuring stained pine, white Carrera marble, and other warm, natural materials. The floor combines wood and colored concrete.

Large openings were created in the wall between the dining room and the retail bakery. Flooring in the bakery consists of ceramic mosaic tiles and shelving is same stained pine featured in the dining area. The retail market theme was carried into an adjacent private dining room featuring historic photos on whitewashed wood walls.

Photography by Douglas Dun, San Francisco, California

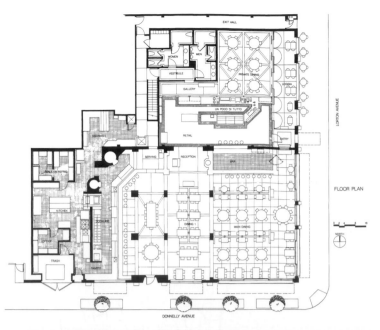

FLOOR PLAN

HONORABLE MENTION

MAISON CUVILLIER

MONTRÉAL

DESIGN
GERVAIS/HARDING ASSOCIATES DESIGN
MONTRÉAL

This 7,600-square-foot historic building connects to a new office building in the heart of old Montreal. The design called for a non-traditional food court due to space configuration and numerous accesses. The space houses food operations of five concessions and 180 seats. Flooring in the older section uses original materials with a combination of gray limestone and irregular slate. A central seating area—featuring a working fireplace—was introduced. While each concession has its own "personality" some finishes, and colors from the public area have been repeated. Custom tiles, wrought iron, carved wood, painted oil cloth, and mosaic copper plating are some examples of finishes used for individual counters.

Photography by Yves Lafebvre, Montréal

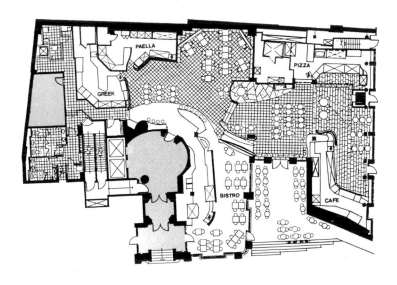

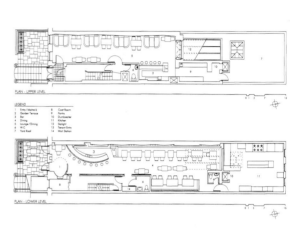

PLAN - UPPER LEVEL

LEGEND

1	Entry/Maitre'd	8	Coat Room
2	Garden Terrace	9	Pantry
3	Bar	10	Dumbwaiter
4	Dining	11	Kitchen
5	Lounge/Dining	12	Skylight
6	W.C.	13	Tenant Entry
7	Yard Roof	14	Wait Station

PLAN - LOWER LEVEL

MASS MERCHANT/DISCOUNT/
MANUFACTURER OUTLET STORE
OR OFF-PRICE

FIRST PLACE

HUSH
PUPPIES
DIRECT

VERO BEACH, FLORIDA

DESIGN
FITCH INC.
WORTHINTON, OHIO

With a commitment of redesigning a new Hush Puppies image, the designers extended this new look into their new store. Materials included maple wood along with a rich palette of earth-toned purples, oranges, browns, and yellows. Four mobile floor fixtures resembling wheelbarrows are featured down the middle of the store—each devoted to one of the company's four product lines. The cashwrap features the same maple at the counter as well as the floor. The children's department, called "Pups," is set off by a floating curved metal sign-band. The merchandising and seating is scaled to a child's size.

Photography by Mark Steele, Fitch Inc., Worthington, Ohio

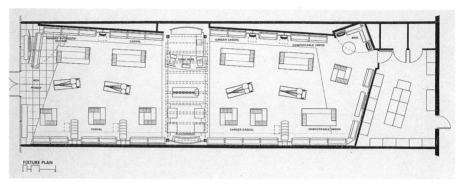

SH PUPPIES & FAMILY DIRECT
lassic
style
walk run play dance
live
TEXTURES
smooth
crisp
bright
deep
rich
colors
simplicity
EARTH'S MOST COMFORTABLE SHO

HONORABLE MENTION

OSHMAN'S SUPERSPORTS USA

SUPER MALL OF THE GREAT NORTHWEST,
AUBURN, WASHINGTON

DESIGN
OSHMAN'S IN-HOUSE PLANNING &
DESIGN TEAM, HOUSTON
IN CONJUNCTION WITH FEOLA CARLI &
ARCHULETA ARCHITECTS
GLENDALE, CALIFORNIA

This 85,000-square-foot store was designed to invoke interactivity through "play areas." Approximately 3,600 square feet is devoted to these areas consisting of basketball and tennis courts, golf area, and batting cage. Ceramic tile aisles circling the sales floor resemble a running course. Other flooring consists of carpet, wood, and vinyl. The ceiling is 22 feet tall to the deck with drop ceilings defining individual departments. The multi-tiered center core, where three aisles converge, features mannequins identifying the fitness, athletic shoe and Nike shop areas.

Photography by Chris Leavitt Photography, Federal Way, Washington

HONORABLE MENTION

HAGGAR OUTLET STORE

THE VILLAGES AT BIRCH RUN, MICHIGAN

DESIGN
FRCH DESIGN WORLDWIDE
CINCINNATI, OHIO

This 4,000-square-foot store reflects the casual attitude of Haggar's new ad campaign, "Stuff You Can Wear." Flooring consists of agglomerate stone tiles and natural wood planks. The ceiling is exposed except for the suspended slabs that define the key areas. A central seating area features open back chairs, a table with a garden hose detail, and a couch shaped like the back of a vintage car. Monitors continuously show music videos interspersed with Haggar commercials. Visual elements and props include bowling balls, tin cans, license plates, old suitcases, billiard balls, and other everyday objects.

Photography by George Cott, Tampa, Florida

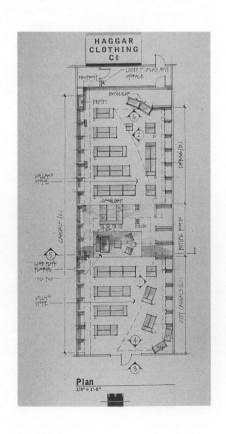

Plan
1/4" = 1'-0"

FIRST PLACE

OPSM 'NEXT'

WESTFIELD SHOPPINGTOWN,
PARRAMATTA, NSW, AUSTRALIA

DESIGN
MARY BRANDON BY DESIGN
PYRMONT, NSW, AUSTRALIA

'Next' is the first prototype of a new boutique concept for OPSM, an optometrist/optical outlet. Fixturing for this 600-square-foot store has been scaled down to fit the space. A joinery fixture was designed with tiered shelving to house a large number of frames. Double-sided lightboxes, adjustable mirrors, four slide-out shelves, and storage were incorporated. The counter and back wall fixtures are furniture pieces, recessed into the curved rear wall of the space. Flooring consists of Jarrah timbers with carpet inlays. Neon lining a ceiling cove casts a cool glow around the perimeter while low voltage white light adds to the clean atmosphere of the small space.

Photography by Adrian Hall, Balmain, Australia

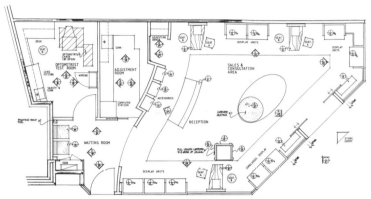

HONORABLE MENTION

CYBERPLAY

UNIVERSITY PARK DRIVE,
WINTER PARK, FLORIDA

DESIGN
KIDS UNLIMITED, INC.
MOUNT DORA, FLORIDA

This store resembles a movie set more than a retail space. Theatrical lighting and day-glow colors combine with burnished steel to create an interior design based on the helm of a postulated 23rd-century starship. The store is divided into five areas: "Byte Size Zone," "Random Access Zone," "Data Base," "Tradeport," and "Buffer Zone." Shown is the "Random Access Zone" including 28 computer workstations created for children ages 7 to 14. The space showcases a unique trussing infrastructure, hovering sound domes, and punched metal backlit baseboards.

Photography by John Petrey, Orlando, Florida

HONORABLE MENTION

MCI CONNECTIONS

THE FASHION CENTRE AT PENTAGON CITY,
ARLINGTON, VIRGINIA

DESIGN
INTERBRAND SCHECHTER
NEW YORK CITY

The designers were commissioned
to create a new brand identity and retail
design for MCI Connections. The logo,
appearing on the storefront as well as on
other materials, incorporates the company's signature orange complemented
with black and blue. The storefront also
features full-height glass windows sur-
rounding an offset entrance. In the windows, suspended bust forms each
advertise a product category. Adjacent
is a polarized "menu-board" fixture out-
lining the product mix. Opposite the
entrance is a nine-screen videowall continuously playing MCI product videos.
Inside, customers are led to the central
fixture that houses telephones—and
offers a free call anywhere throughout
the world.

Photography by Andrew Bordwin, New York City

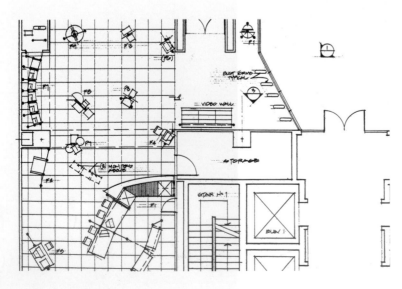

FIRST PLACE

CADBURY KIOSK

MELBOURNE CENTRAL SHOPPING CENTRE,
VICTORIA, AUSTRALIA

DESIGN
SYNTHESIS DESIGN & DISPLAY PTY. LTD.
VICTORIA, AUTRALIA

The design objective was to project the company image, branding, and product at all times from every direction. Design dictated that the kiosk go from storage mode to operational mode in short order. Medium-density fiberboard was the construction material chosen to best project the design intentions including the fabrication of the chocolate replica. The counter is self-contained and rides on a rolling carriage for easy mobility. Soft corners were incorporated to make the kiosk approachable at many angles. Auto paint gives the unit a highly polished, clean appearance.

Photography by Gary Lewis Photography, Melbourne, Australia

HONORABLE MENTION

NEW WORLD COFFEE

RIVERSIDE SQUARE MALL,
HACKENSACK, NEW JERSEY

DESIGN
RONNETTE RILEY ARCHITECT
NEW YORK CITY

The design objective was to translate the interior of New World Coffee's shop to a freestanding pavilion. Earth colors of cherry wood, copper-toned bronze, and black steel from New World's shops are incorporated into the kiosk design. Angled bronze columns and glass display cabinets mark the corners of the structure, while flooring of Rosa Aura marble is inlaid with terra-cotta veining. Angular pendant light fixtures hang above the counter highlighting the custom bronze work and accent panels. Open to the skylit atrium above, the kiosk is visible from all levels of the mall.

Photography by Dub Rogers, New York City

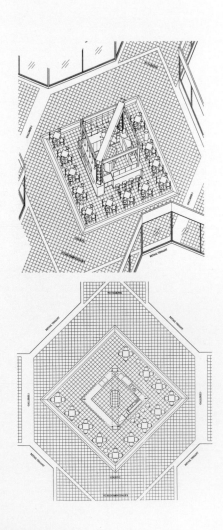

HONORABLE MENTION

NEWS TRAVELS

LOGAN INTERNATIONAL AIRPORT,
BOSTON, MASSACHUSETTS

DESIGN
FIORINO DESIGN, INC.
TORONTO, CANADA

The design challenge was to create an airport kiosk unique to the Boston and New England area. An open overhead system of straight and curved metal trusses was engineered as an overall canopy, with track lighting secured to the underside of the metal trusses. Two-tone faux stone-clad columns support the canopy and enclose the sliding grilles that secure the retail space when not in use. The neutral palette is warm sandy taupe and gray in polished and unpolished textures. Wall and floor fixtures, constructed of plastic laminate and high-density fiberboard, are on wheels for easy mobility.

Photography by Design Archive, Toronto

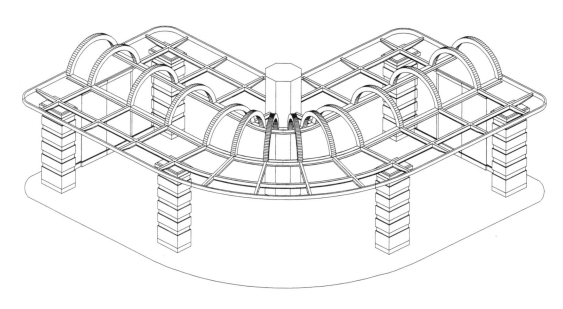

AXONOMETRIC OF KIOSK

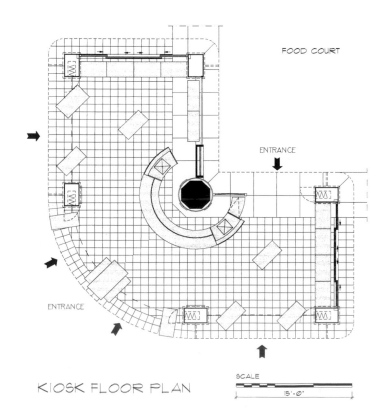

FOOD COURT

ENTRANCE

ENTRANCE

KIOSK FLOOR PLAN

SCALE

15'-0"

TEMPUS EXPEDITIONS

MALL OF AMERICA,
BLOOMINGTON, MINNESOTA

DESIGN
FRCH DESIGN WORLDWIDE
CINCINNATI, OHIO

This 6,000-square-foot store offers a combination of entertainment and education in a themed environment. The storefront features a larger-than-life, three-dimensional figure with one foot in the mall and the other inside the store. The vibrant colors and bright yellow neon lighting are designed to attract passersby. Inside, giant gears hang from the entry ceiling and are reflected in the pattern of the terrazzo flooring below. The column to the right of the entrance is decorated with watch parts, gears, and mechanical inventions. To the left is a 2,300-square-foot retail area designed to capture customers before and after they experience the motion simulator ride.

Photography by Dan Forer, Miami

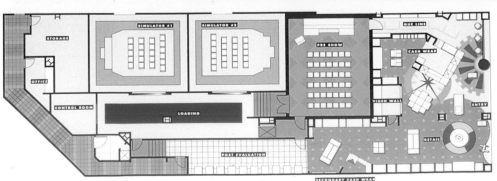

BIG FUTURE INTERACTIVE THEME HOUSE

CLAYTON ROAD,
ST. LOUIS, MISSOURI

DESIGN
KIKU OBATA & COMPANY, INC.
ST. LOUIS, MISSOURI

This 13,000-square-foot space features virtual reality, CD-ROM, and high-tech video games. Design incorporates larger-than-life kiosk fixtures, each featuring a different interactive computer game or adventure. Designed to easily accommodate changes and new technology, the fixtures are fabricated of MDF with a high-gloss automotive lacquer, with metal, foam, and plastic laminates. The retail store features fixtures of clear finished maple. A "Main Street" aisle of ceramic tile and inlaid geometric inserts leads visitors through the store to exhibits and eventually to the open plaza snack bar.

Photography by Alise O'Brien, St. Louis

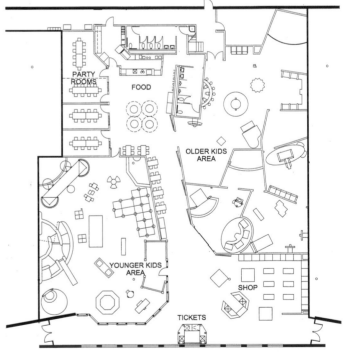

REGAL CINEMAS FUNSCAPE

JARMIN ROAD, CHESAPEAKE, VIRGINIA

DESIGN
INTERIOR SYSTEMS, INC. (ISI)
FOND DU LAC, WISCONSIN

Walking into the Toy Box transforms the ordinary child and parent into a participant. The Crayon Storage Unit, Supersize Scribble Pad Memo Board, Thematic Artist Palette Table, and Paint Jar Seats, Coral Reef Decor for Interactive Seas are products designed to create interactive opportunities for children and parents.

The "Interactive Seas Bubble Column" archway and "Gamemania" archway define key attractions in the play area. These archways, with their vibrant colors and miniature game parts, initiate visitors to find new adventures within the FunScape complex.

Photography by Curtis K. Bias, Virginia Beach, Virginia

FIRST PLACE

JHANE BARNES INC.

WEST 57TH STREET,
NEW YORK CITY

DESIGN
MATSUYAMA INTERNATIONAL CORP.
NEW YORK CITY

Jhane Barnes' reception counter features curved frosted glass on both sides with columns connecting to beams in the ceiling. An open space leads to the stairs and atrium space. Mirrors are displayed on both sides of the 50-foot high atrium walls. Concrete flooring with a stained finish compliments the brushed steel and mesh screen display units.

Photography by Paul Warchol Photography,
New York City

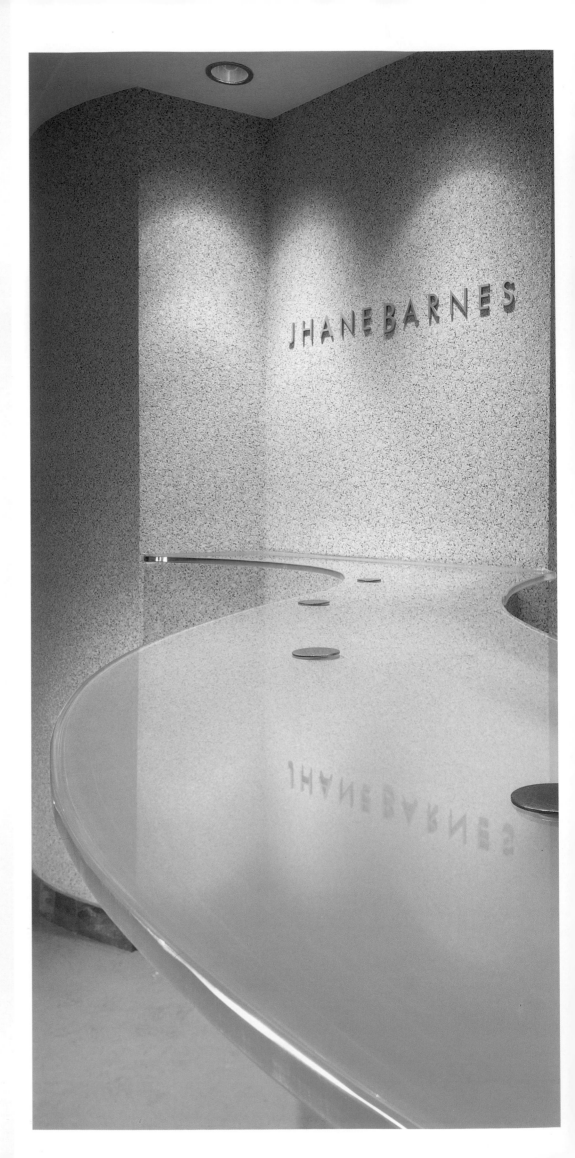

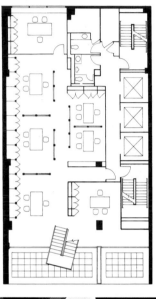
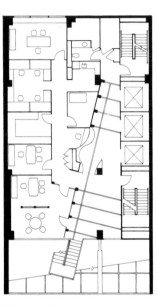

HONORABLE MENTION

CLARENCE HOUSE

SAN FRANCISCO, CALIFORNIA

DESIGN
EVA MADDOX ASSOCIATES INC.
CHICAGO, ILLINOIS

The architecture for this 10,000-square-foot design center created an environmental backdrop for the display of textiles. External building materials are seen in the interior with structural lighting and occasional brick walls. Design features include the raw wood beams, natural wood ceiling, and wrought-iron lighting system. Wrought iron also appears in the fixturing. This symmetrical floor plan allows for maximum efficiency.

Photography by Steve Hall of Hedrich Blessing, Chicago

HONORABLE MENTION

QUANTUM AT COMDEX

LAS VEGAS CONVENTION CENTER

DESIGN
SHEA ARCHITECTS, INC.
MINNEAPOLIS, MINNESOTA

Designed for trade show use, this 4,200-square-foot exhibit can be reconfigured for reuse. Designed to communicate changes in storage technology, the exhibit's materials supported the idea with corrugated fiberglass, plexiglass and plywood. A large billboard hung over the exhibit, creating a presence from any perspective. The reception desk, shown, is constructed of sandblasted aluminum supports, perforated metal panels, and frosted plexiglass. Props and decoratives were salvaged items such as computers, appliances, ladders, and mannequins.

Photography by Sinclair Reinsch, Mike Sinclair

PLAZA JEWELERS

SANTA ROSA PLAZA, CALIFORNIA

DESIGN
MIROGLIO ARCHITECTURE + DESIGN
OAKLAND, CALIFORNIA

Plaza Jewelers' space is intended to communicate the idea of a giant jewelry box. Curving exterior walls are covered with custom maple panels, attached with jewelery-like custom metal fasteners. Jewelry touches on signage include gold and silver finishes and diamond-prong fasteners on mahogany accent bands. Even the custom stools are shaped like miniature jewelry boxes—which, when opened, reveal velvet-covered seat cushions. Providing a focus for the space is a maple panel display wall that serves as a backdrop to the "Design Center" in the rear of the store, where clients can customize settings for jewels via a three-dimensional computer program.

Photography by Alan Weintraub, San Francisco

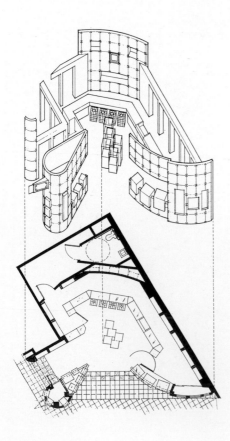

HONORABLE MENTION

TIFFANY & CO.

THE MALL AT SHORT HILLS,
NEW JERSEY

DESIGN
TIFFANY & CO. STORE PLANNING & DESIGN
NEW YORK CITY

The designers took inspiration and details from Tiffany's New York City flagship, including the signature granite that covers its entry arch. In this particular store, the facade is constructed of Italian sandstone within a columned framework of Texas limestone. Inside, on the right, two custom cherry vitrines anchor the mirrored wall treatment framed in stainless steel. To the left, two marbled portals lead to the "Tabletop" and "Accessories Salon." Neutral colors, such as cream colored silk wall fabrics, compliment showcases of warm cherry wood and marble. Showcase bases and stone countertops match the marble portal treatments. The store is illuminated by fluorescents in the curved ceiling cove with accent lighting supplied by recessed downlights.

Photography by Briskey Photography, Hinsdale, Illinois

HONORABLE MENTION

TIFFANY & CO.

THE WESTCHESTER,
WHITE PLAINS, NEW YORK

DESIGN
TIFFANY & CO. STORE PLANNING & DESIGN
NEW YORK CITY

Italian granite and Texas limestone materials were again selected for the facade to compliment the mall's color palette. The signature granite entry arch is incorporated also in a round-top version for the windows. At the entrance of the 1,500-square-foot store, runs of showcases offer a clear sense of direction. Walls feature framed prints of original artwork of historical jewelry designs from the company's past. Flower arrangements in vases add a splash of color to this neutral palette. Lighting is provided by ceiling cove fluorescents and by directional and fixed downlights with MR-16 lamps.

Photography by Briskey Photography, Hinsdale, Illinois

62 SAM GOODY

HORTON PLAZA, SAN DIEGO

Design: Musicland Group, Inc., Minnetonka, Minn.—Jack Eugster, president; John Myklebust, managing director design and architecture; Rick Bateson, director of construction; Todd Young, architecture project manager; Joe Darin, construction project manager; **Designer:** The Jerde Partnership, Venice, Calif.; David Glover, project manager; **Architect:** RSP Architects, Minneapolis, Michael Plautz, partner-in-charge; Bill Wittrock, project manager; **Architectural Lighting:** Joe Kaplan, Los Angeles; **General Contractor:** Johnson & Jennings, San Diego, Jackie Jennings; **Fixturing:** Musicland Group, Inc., Minnetonka, Minn.; **Furniture:** Musicland Group, Inc., Minnetonks, Minn. **Flooring:** Progressive Concrete, Escondido, Calif. (concrete finish) **Lighting:** West Philadelphia Electric, Philadelphia; Lighting Services, Inc., Minneapolis (gooseneck fixtures); **Wall Coverings:** Perma Groove, Lakeville, Minn. (slotted wallboard); **Signage:** Clearr Corp., Minnetonka, Minn. (light boxes); Fluoresco, Phoenix (exterior signs); **Props/Decoratives:** Peter Carlson Enterprises, Sun Valley, Calif. (angel, cherub, toy and interior column); **Special Equipment:** Otis Elevator, San Diego (elevator); Impart, Inc., Seattle (TV brackets); Coast Restaurant Supply, LaMesa, Calif. (kitchen equipment); Gold Coast Coffee Carts, San Diego (espresso machine and grinder)

70 BRUNO'S SUPERCENTER

SANDY SPRINGS PLACE, ATLANTA

Design: Programmed Products Corp., Plymouth, Mich.—Llew Reszka, president; John Zafarana, CEO; **Architect:** Garrison-Barrett Group, Birmingham, Ala.; **General Contractor:** H.J. Russell Construction Co., Atlanta; **Fixturing:** Madix Store Fixtures, Terrell, Texas (metal gondolas); Southern Store Fixtures, Inc., Bessemer, Ala. (custom millwork and perishables displays); **Flooring:** Armstrong World Ind. Inc., Lancaster, Pa. (VCT/sales floor); Azrock Industries, Inc., San Antonio, Texas (slip-resistant VCT/sales floor); American Olean Tile Corp., Lansdale, Pa. (public restrooms); Buchtal Corp., USA, Roswell, Ga. (service prep areas); **Ceiling:** Armstrong World Ind. Inc., Lancaster, Pa. (service area, lay-in ceiling systems); **Lighting:** Lithonia Hi-Tek Industrial & Commercial Lighting Corp., Crawfordsville, Ind. (H.I.D. lighting); Columbia Lighting Corp., Spokane, Wash. (recessed fluorescent); Amerlux Corp., Fairfield, N.J. (HQI); Kichler Lighting, Cleveland (pendant fixtures); Accentrak (NL Corp.), Cleveland (low-voltage lighting); Hartford Lighting, Manchester, Conn. (pendant style fixtures); **Signage:** Barnes Quality Signs, Inc., Acworth, Ga. (neon tube and neon channel letters); Custom Photo Art, Birmingham, Ala. (photomural production); **All Other Decor & Signage:** Programmed Products Corp., Plymouth, Mich.; **Awning:** Awning Engineering Corp., Kennesaw, Ga.; **Special Equipment:** Hussmann Corp., Bridgeton, Mo. (refrigeration); Arneg Co., Nazareth, Pa. (refrigeration)

74 VIC'S WORLD CLASS MARKET

GRAND RIVER AVE., NOVI, MICH.

Sign Design: Programmed Products Corp., Plymouth, Mich.—Llew Reszka, president; John Zafarana, CEO; **Architecture and Interiors:** Jon Sarkesian Architects, P.C., Royal Oak, Mich.; **Fixturing:** Puma Construction, Redford, Mich.; **Flooring:** Indus Ceramic Tile, Modena, Italy; **Ceiling:** Chicago Metallic Corp., Chicago; **Lighting:** Rejuvenation Lamp & Fixture Co., Portland, Ore.; **Laminates:** Formica, Cincinnati; Nevamar, Odenton, Md.; **Fabrics:** Robert Allen Fabrics, Mansfield, Mass.; Belle Isle Awning, Roseville, Mich.; **Signage:** Programmed Products Corp. Plymouth, Mich.; Planet Neon Sign Co., Novi, Mich.; **Materials:** Decorator's Supply Corp., Chicago (ornamental wood); W.F. Norman Corp., Nevada, Mo. (ornamental metal); Fypon Molded Millwork, Stewartstown, Pa. (architectural foam molding); **Special Equipment:** Keyes Refrigeration, Livonia, Mich.; **Photographer:** Llew Reszka, Plymouth, Mich.

78 LIQUOR CONTROL BOARD OF ONTARIO

QUEEN STREET EAST, TORONTO

Design: The International Design Group, Toronto—Ronald Harris, president; David Newman, manager-in-charge; Andrew Gallici, designer; Ron Mazereeuw, job captain; **Liquor Control Board of Ontario Design Team:** Jackie Bonic, director of store development and real estate; Tino Caguiat, design coordinator; John Jensen, construction manager; Fred Clark, construction coordinator; **General Contractor:** BMG Enterprises, Mississauga, Ont.; **Fixturing:** BMG Enterprises, Mississauga, Ont.; **Flooring:** Forbo, Toronto; **Lighting:** Juno Lighting, Toronto; **Wall Coverings:** Antonio Cangemi, Toronto (artist); Murad (mural/artist)

82 IL FORNAIO

BURLINGAME, CALIF.

Design: Backen Arrigoni & Ross, Inc., San Francisco—Howard Backen, principal; Kenneth Catton, project architect; Bumps Baldauf, kitchen designer; **Architect:** Backen Arrigoni & Ross Inc., San Francisco; **General Contractor:** C.J. Torre Construction, El Cajon, Calif.; **Furniture:** West Coast Industries, San Francisco (tables); F.W. Lombard, Ashburnham, Mass. (chairs); **Flooring:** D & J Tile, Redwood City, Calif.; **Lighting:** Neidhardt, San Francisco; **Signage:** Polachek, San Rafael, Calif.; AdArt, Oakland, Calif.; **Millwork:** Adams Tailored Woodworking, Newark, Calif.; **Displays:** Skeleton Crew Design, San Rafael, Calif.

88 MAISON CUVILLIER

OSTELL, MONTREAL

Design: Gervais Harding Associes Design, Montreal—Denis Gervais, president; Irene Harding and Frank DiNiro, design and design development; James Lee, technical development; **Maison Cuvillier Design Team:** Pierre Paquin, project director; Tom Fullum, planning; **General Contractor:** Conception CAMA, Montreal; **Flooring:** Ciot, Montreal; Céragérs, Montreal; **Lighting:** Futura, Montreal; Corlite, Montreal; **Woodwork:** Perfectart, Montreal; **Finishes:** Faux Et Usage De Faux, Montreal; Naomi Pearl, Montreal; **Metal Work:** Lucifer, Montreal

92 LEX

EAST 65TH STREET, NEW YORK CITY

Owner: Henry Lambert; **Design:** Edward I. Mills & Associates, New York City—Edward Mills, principal; Jeff McKean, project manager; **Architect:** Edward I. Mills & Associates, New York City; **General Contractor:** Cook & Krupa, New York City; **Lighting Consultant:** Kruger Associates, New York City, Mark Kruger; **Fixtures:** Downtown Interiors, New York City; **Furniture:** Chairs & Stools Inc., New York City (chairs and stools); **Flooring:** Consolidated Carpet, New York City; **Wall Coverings:** Beriah Wall, New York City (plaster); **Fabrics:** Kirk Brummel, New York City; **Signage:** Lebowitz-Gould, New York City

94 HUSH PUPPIES DIRECT

VERO BEACH, FLA.

Design: Fitch Inc., Worthington, Ohio—Martin Beck, CEO; Jaimie Alexander, vice president; P. Kelly Mooney, vice president; Doug Smith, director; Alycia Freeman; director; Kian Kuan director; Randy Miller, senior associate; **Hush Puppies Design Team:** Blaine Jungers, president; Dave Bonney, director; **General Contractor:** Jaycon Development, Memphis, Tenn.; **Fixturing:** Mock Woodworking Company, Zanesville, Ohio; **Flooring:** Monterey Carpet, Santa Ana, Calif. (carpet); Toli CTS Flooring, Limerick, Pa. (vinyl); Design Materials, Kansas City, Kan. (vinyl); Interface Retail Flooring, Cartersville, Ga. (vinyl); **Lighting:** Lighting Management, Inc. New City, N.Y. (lighting elements); **Laminates:** Wilsonart, Temple, Texas; **Wall Coverings:** Benjamin Moore, Montvale, N.J. (paint); Glidden, Cleveland (paint); **Signage & Graphics:** Chroma Studios, Columbus, Ohio (signage graphics, production); T&T Label, Miamisburg, Ohio (POP signage, production)

98 OSHMAN'S SUPERSPORTS USA

SUPER MALL OF THE GREAT NORTHWEST, AUBURN, WASH.

Design: Oshman's In-house Planning and Design Team in conjunction with Feola Carli & Archuleta Architects, Glendale, Calif.—Marilyn Oshman, chair; Alvin Lubetken, CEO and vice chairman; Bill Anderson, president and COO; **Oshman's Design Team:** Chris Lauritzen, director of store planning and construction; RoxAnna A. Sway, ISP, director of creative services and visual merchandising; Robert McBrinn, project manager; Nabs Carlson, visual merchandising coordinator; Reggie Gray, visual merchandising coordinator; **Consulting Architects:** Feola Carli & Archuleta Architects, Andrew Feola, AIA, principal-in-charge; Luis Cota, ISP, planner; Wesley Ashby, AIA, project team; Gisela Riobueno, project team; **General Contractor:** Robert E. Bayley Construction, Inc., Seattle; **Fixturing:** Famous Fixtures, SunPrarie, Wis. (wood); ABC/Spectrum, New York City (metal); Crystalon, Commerce, Calif. (specialty); Robelon Display, Hempstead, N.Y. (specialty); Nike, Inc., Lisle, Ill. (vendor); Columbia Sportswear Company, Portland, Ore. (vendor); Woolrich, Inc., Woolrich, Pa. (vendor); Roll-It, Inc. Lachine, Canada (perimeter wall fixtures); **Flooring:** Lotus Carpet, Columbus, Ga. (carpet); Dal-Tile, Dallas (ceramic tile); Panel Specialists, Inc., Temple, Texas (wood flooring, basketball court); PermaGrain Products, Inc., Media, Pa. (center court); Lonseal, Inc., Carson, Calif. (vinyl); **Ceiling & Trim:** U.S.G. (Compasso), Chicago; **Lighting:** Holophane, Columbus, Ohio; **Laminates:** Wilsonart, Temple, Texas; Interlam, Inc., Fort Lauderdale, Fla.; **Signage & Graphics:** KMDI, Kansas City, Kan.; 3-M, Minneapolis (floor graphics); **Mannequins:** Greneker, Los Angeles; **Other Materials:** Firebird Industries, New Orleans (timberposts) Specialty Equipment: Sport Court, Houston (exercise mats and in-line skate matting); Western Golf, Thousand Palms, Calif. (golf club racks); Power Alley, Lilburn, Ga. (batting cage simulator); Full Swing Golf, Poway, Calif. (golf simulator); York Barbell, York, Pa. (barbell fixtures); Impart, Inc., Seattle (video wall)

102 HAGGAR OUTLET STORE

THE VILLAGES AT BIRCH RUN, MICH.

Design: FRCH Design Worldwide, Cincinnati—James Fitzgerald, chair and CEO; Kevin Roche, partner-in-charge; Joan Donnelly, principal-in-charge; Robert Rutledge, design director; Caryn Keller, senior designer; Tessa Westermeyer, creative director; Chip Williamson, project architect; Pamela Dull, architect; Carole Mahan, visual merchandiser; Cynthia Turner, lighting designer; Gerry Power, lighting designer; Inez Baird, CPM designer; **Haggar Design Team:** Joseph Haggar III, ceo; Frank Bracken, president and coo; Alan Burks, senior vice president marketing; Ron Batts, vice president Haggar Direct; Tracey Altman, manager media relations; Bill Jasper, store operations manager; Kira Schmidt, merchandise coordinator; **General Contractor:** Price-Woods, Mesa, Ariz.; **Fixturing:** MET Merchandising Concepts, Chicago; Hamilton Fixtures, Cincinnati (sign holders); **Furniture:** T.O.M.T., New York City; Pastense, San Francisco; Beverly, Pico Rivera, Calif.; **Flooring:** Quarella, Ontario, Canada (tile); Karastan Bigelow, Philadelphia (carpet); PermaGrain, Media, Pa. (wood); **Lighting:** Abolite, Cincinnati; Hubbel Lighting Inc., Christiansburg, Va.; Juno Lighting Inc., Des Plaines, Ill.; Lightolier, Secaucus, N.J.; Lithonia, Decatur, Ga.; Time Square Lighting, Stony Point, N.Y.; **Finishes:** Forbo Industries, Hazleton, Pa.; Ardmore Textured Metals Inc., Edison, N.J.; Ben Rose Ltd., Grand Rapids, Mich.; Spinney Beck, Amherst, N.Y.; Putnam Rolling Ladder Co., New York City; **Signage:** PLI, Cincinnati (restroom/fitting room signs); Adex, Cincinnati (cloth banners); **Decoratives:** Precision Digital, Cincinnati (framed photos); Photographic Specialties, New York City (large-scale photos)

106 OPSM 'NEXT'

WESTFIELD SHOPPINGTOWN, PARRAMATTA, AUSTRALIA

Design: Mary Brandon By Design, Pyrmont, Australia—Mary Brandon, president and designer; Allan Griffiths, project manager; **OPSM 'Next' Design Team:** Glynis Wood, marketing director; Brian Jones, construction manager; **General Contractor:** Original Displays, Sydney, Australia; **Fixturing:** Mary Brandon By Design, Pyrmont, Australia (designed fixtures); Original Displays, Sydney, Australia (manufactured); **Flooring:** Bremworth, Sydney, Australia; **Ceiling:** Mary Brandon By Design, Pyrmont, Australia (designed); Original Displays, Sydney, Australia (installed); **Lighting:** Reggiani, Sydney, Australia (installed); **Wall Coverings:** Original Displays, Sydney, Australia **Fabrics:** Halifax, Sydney, NSW, Australia (Amara); **Signage:** Prelite Neon, Sydney, Australia

110 CYBERPLAY

UNIVERSITY PARK DRIVE, WINTER PARK, FLA.

Design: Kids Unlimited, Inc., Mount Dora, Fla.—Steven Shamrock, CEO and co-chair; Susan Ray, president and co-chair; Jack Bush, vice chairman; Ron Young, senior vice president development and construction; Bruce Lagravinese, chief information officer and director of marketing; Amy Shamrock, vice president of real estate services; Trisha Eckoff, design consultant; Pamela Mazey, center manager; Frank Vigil, INTEL Corp.'s retail PC channel manager; **Architect:** Alan Farrar, Orlando, Fla.; **General Contractor:** The Gainsborough Group, Inc., Orlando, Fla.; **Fixturing:** Excell Stores Fixtures Inc., Toronto; **Furniture:** Eckes Associates, Inc. (chairs); **Flooring:** Durkan Carpets, Dalton, Ga. (carpet); American Floor Products Co., Rockville, Md. (rubber); Pro Source Of Orlando, Orlando, Fla. (rubber); **Ceiling:** Brown Innovations, Inc., Chicago (sound domes); **Lighting:** Villa Lighting Supply, St. Louis; **Laminates:** Wilsonart, Temple, Texas; **Wall Coverings:** Orlando Plastics, Inc., Winter Springs, Fla. **Signage:** Orlando Plastics Inc., Winter Springs, Fla. (exterior); Wace Imaging Network, Orlando, Fla. (interior); Next Day Signs, Longwood, Fla. (interior); **Specialty Equipment:** United Sales, Ocala, Fla. (restroom fixtures); Koala Corp., St. Paul, Minn. (baby changing tables); American Covers Inc., Draper, Utah (mouse pads); Audio Coll Corp., Miami (televisions); CDS Alarm System, Deland, Fla. (security)

114 MCI CONNECTIONS

THE FASHION CENTRE AT PENTAGON CITY, ARLINGTON, VA.

Design: Interbrand Schechter, New York City—Charles Brymer, president; David Wales, vice president creative director retail branding; Brent Robertson, designer; **MCI Connections Design Team:** Robert Gay, senior manager; Laura Bollettino, manager cellular marketing; **Fixtures/Forms:** Alu, New York City; WMA, Brooklyn, N.Y.; Superior Architectural, Queens, N.Y.

116 CADBURY KIOSK

MELBOURNE CENTRAL SHOPPING CENTRE, VICTORIA, AUSTRALIA

Design: Synthesis Design & Display Pty Ltd., Victoria, Australia—Jason Laity, design director; Les Laity, project director; **Cadbury Schweppes Design Team:** Peter Beales, marketing manager Cadbury Schweppes Confectionery Division; **Lighting:** Retail Lighting Systems, Melbourne, Australia; **Flooring:** Boral Timber, Melbourne, Australia (hardwood); **Signage:** Gadsden Signs Australia, Melbourne, Australia (neon); **Materials:** M&T Allison, Melbourne, Australia (metal work); **Props/Decoratives:** Synthesis Design & Display Pty Ltd Production Team

118 NEW WORLD COFFEE

RIVERSIDE SQUARE MALL, HACKENSACK, N.J.

Design: Ronnette Riley Architect, New York City—Ronnette Riley, principal; Dale Turner, project architect; Scott Springer and Sarah Hargreaves Shields, project managers; **General Contractor:** Richter + Ratner Contracting Group, Maspeth, N.Y.; **Fixturing:** Modelsmith, Hoboken, N.J. (custom cabinetry); Richter + Ratner Contracting Group, Maspeth, N.Y. (custom cabinetry); **Furniture:** Gullen Int'l., New York City ("Tokyo" stools); **Lighting:** Leucos, Edison, N.J. ("Star 14"); Indy Lighting, Fishers, Ind. (track); **Signage:** Philadelphia Sign Company, Palmyra, N.J.; **Ornamental Metalwork:** Modelsmith, Hoboken, N.J.

120 NEWS TRAVELS

LOGAN INTERNATIONAL AIRPORT, BOSTON

Design: Fiorino Design Inc., Toronto—Nella Fiorino, design principal and project manager; Vilija Gacionis and Miodrag Antic, designers; **Client:** Allders International U.S.A., Canada; **General Contractor:** Bonfatti, Norwood, Mass.; **Fixturing:** Pancor Industries Ltd., Mississauga, Ont.; **Flooring:** Ferleo Tile Inc., Rexdale, Ont.; **Lighting:** Halo, Elk Grove Village, Ill.; **Laminates:** Arborite, La Salle, Que.; Wilsonart, Temple, Texas; **Paint Finishes:** P.C.U. Coatings, Toronto; **Signage:** Sunset Neon, Toronto; **Graphic Designer:** Taylor & Browning, Toronto

124 TEMPUS EXPEDITIONS

MALL OF AMERICA, BLOOMINGTON, MINN.

Design: FRCH Design Worldwide, Cincinnati — James Fitzgerald, chairman and CEO; Kevin Roche, partner-in-charge; Mike Beeghly, principal-in-charge; Steve McGowan, senior project designer; Tom Horwitz, project director; Romano Klepec, production assistant; Chip Williamson, production assistant; Laina Bogner, design assistant; Laura Lee, graphic designer; Les Bradford, production assistant; **Tempus Expeditions Design Team:** William Sadleir, president; Rosalind Nowicki, co-director of merchandise; Linda Irvin, co-director of merchandise; Kimcee McAnally, director of organizational development; **General Contractor:** Fortney & Weygandt, Lakewood, Ohio; **Fixturing:** JPM, Eden Prairie, Minn.; Siewert, Minneapolis; **Flooring:** Bentley, Oklahoma City (carpet); Mannington Commercial, Calhoun, Ga. (tile); Toli Int'l., Commack, N.Y. (tile); Forbo, Hazleton, Pa.; Viking Terrazzo Company, Minneapolis (terrazzo); **Lighting:** Lighting Management Inc., New City, N.Y.; **Special Finish:** Marlite, Dover, Ohio; **Wall Coverings:** Archetonic, Yonkers, N.Y.; Blumenthal, Long Island City, N.Y.; Anya Larkin, New York City; Innovations, New York City; **Fabrics:** Unika Vaev, Orangeburg, N.Y.; HBF Textiles, Long Island City, N.Y.; HGH Design Group, San Francisco; **Signage and Graphics:** Kieffer & Co., Marietta, Ga. (storefront); 3M, Minneapolis (graphics on storefront); Sterling, Cincinnati (fixture logo fabricator); **Special Equipment:** Moog Inc., East Aurora, N.Y. (simulator); Triad Systems, Des Moines, Iowa (show control); Sony Electronics, Montvale, N.J. (high definition visual); High Performance Stereo, Boston (surround sound); Dream Quest Images, Simi Valley, Calif. (film production); Blumberg Communications, Minneapolis (projection screens) M-E Engineering Inc., Columbus, Ohio (engineers)

128 BIG FUTURE — INTERACTIVE THEME HOUSE

ST. LOUIS

Design: Kiku Obata & Company, Inc., St. Louis — Kiku Obata, principal; Gen Obata, designer; Rich Nelson, designer; Tim McGinty, architect; Jane McNeely, graphic designer; James Keane, architect; Theresa Henrekin, designer; **General Contractor:** Alberici Construction Company, St. Louis; **Fixturing:** Design Fabricators, Boulder, Colo.; **Lighting:** Randy Burkett Lighting Design, St. Louis; **Signage:** Engravings Unlimited, St. Louis

132 REGAL CINEMAS FUNSCAPE

CHESAPEAKE, VA.

Design: Interior Systems, Inc., Fond du Lac, Wis.— Lindsey S. Bovinet, president and CEO; Scott Swick, vice president sales and marketing; Rhonda L. P. Hoffmann, entertainment account executive; Scott Steffen, project manager; Amy Lucas, senior interior designer; Bonnie Ann Gleason Federman, art director and studio production supervisor; Kathy Beilfuss, graphic designer; Richard Treleven, project estimator; Mark Huck, director of manufacturing; Steve Emmer, field service supervisor; Richard Roman, concept developer; **Concept Design:** Bruce D. Robinson, Architecture-Design Inc., Cincinnati — Bruce Robinson, principal-in-charge; Randy Vuksta, project architect; Mark Snell, project designer; **Architect:** Atkinson/ Dyer/Watson Architects; Michael Dyer, partner-in-charge; Robert Lauer, associate partner-in-charge; Tim Cohen, project architect; **General Contractor:** Ediface, Inc., Charlotte, N.C.; **Flooring:** American Olean, Tampa, Fla.; Crossville Ceramics, Crossville, Tenn.; Shaw Carpets, Dalton, Ga.; Cumberland Mills, Vineland, N.J.; Atlas Carpet Mills, Los Angeles; All State Rubber Tile, Ozone Park, N.Y.; **Ceiling:** Armstrong Tile, Lancaster, Pa.; **Laminates:** Wilsonart, Temple, Texas; Nevamar, Odenton, Md.; Formica, Cincinnati; Pionite, Auburn, Maine; **Wall Coverings:** Genon, Hackensack, N.J.; Seabrook, Memphis, Tenn.; Koroseal, Fairlawn, Ohio; JM Lynne, Louisville, Ky. **Fabrics:** Boltaflex, Temperance, Mich.; **Signage & Graphics:** Interior Systems, Inc., Fond du Lac, Wis.; East Coast Signs, Bristol, Pa.; **Props/Decoratives:** Interior Systems, Inc., Fond du Lac, Wis.

134 JHANE BARNES INC.

WEST 57TH ST., NEW YORK CITY

Design: Matsuyama Int'l. Corp., New York City — Yoshinari Matsuyama, president; Yasuko Mayuzumi and Yoshinari Matsuyama, managers-in-charge; **Architect:** Albert Arencibia, N.J.; **General Contractor:** Accord Construction Inc., New York City; **Fixturing:** Landmark Architectural Metal and Glass Inc., New York City (metal and glazing); **Stairs:** Newco Iron Works, Ltd., New York City; **Furniture:** Barnhart, Lenior, N.C. (sofa and glass tables); Knoll Studio, Greenville, Pa. (chairs); **Flooring:** Ardex, Inc., New York City; Russ Van Peterson, New York City (custom floor finish); Lester Lockwood, New York City (slate); **Lighting:** Edison Price Lighting, New York City; Elliptipar, West Haven, Conn.; Halo Lighting, Secaucus, N.J.; **Laminates:** Abet Inc., New York City; **Wall Coverings:** Knoll Textile, Greenville, Pa.; **Signage:** Big Apple Corp., New York City; **Mannequins:** Ronis Bros., New York City

138 CLARENCE HOUSE

SAN FRANCISCO

Design: Eva Maddox Associates Inc., Chicago — Eva Maddox, president; Patrick Grzybek, project manager; Eileen Jones, director of design, Keith Curtis, designer; Linda Pollari, designer; **General Contractor:** C.C.I. Construction, San Francisco; **Custom Metal:** West Edge, San Francisco (custom metal work); **Custom Cabinetry:** Pacassa Studios, Oakland, Calif. (custom cabinetry and desks); **Furniture:** Thomas Moser, Portland, Maine (custom seating); **Lighting:** Trimble House, Norcross, Ga. (pendant lights); Cole Lighting, South El Monte, Calif. (suspended lighting)

142 QUANTUM AT COMDEX

LAS VEGAS CONVENTION CENTER

Design: Shea Architects, Inc., Minneapolis — David Shea, president; Gregory Rothweiler, design director; William Hickey, senior project director; Kelly Roemhildt, project architect; **Architect:** Gregory Rothweiler, Minneapolis

144 PLAZA JEWELERS

SANTA ROSA PLAZA, SANTA ROSA, CALIF.

Design: Miroglio Architecture and Design, Oakland, Calif. — Joel Miroglio, principal; **General Contractor:** Swain Nobles Associates, Santa Rosa, Calif.; **Fixturing:** Magic Glass, San Francisco (display fixtures); **Furniture:** Miroglio Architecture and Design, Oakland, Calif. (design); Magic Glass, San Francisco; **Flooring:** Atlas Carpet, City of Commerce, Calif. (carpet); **Lighting:** Halo Lighting, San Francisco; **Laminates:** Formica, Cincinnati; Abet Laminati, Redwood City, Calif.; **Signage:** Real Enterprises, Santa Rosa, Calif.

148 TIFFANY & CO.

THE MALL AT SHORTHILLS, N.J.

Design: Tiffany & Co. Store Planning & Design Department, New York City — Philip Bottega, AIA, vice president; Edward Sullivan, manager of construction; Mark Looper, AIA, store designer; Robin Buckwalter, director of visual merchandising; **Lighting Designer:** Martin Shaffer & Associates, Hoboken, N.J.; **Architect:** JPV Design Group, New York City; **General Contractor:** Planned Management Construction, New York City; **Fixturing:** Modern Woodcrafts, Inc., Farmington, Conn.; **Furniture:** Baker, Knapp & Tubbs, New York City; Manheim Weitz, Dallas; **Flooring:** Designweave, Los Angeles (carpet); **Lighting:** Reggiani USA, Inc., New Windsor, N.Y.; **Laminates:** Wilsonart, Temple, Texas; **Wall Coverings:** Tandem Contract, Inc., Monmoth Junction, N.J.; **Fabrics:** Clarence House, New York City, (upholstery); Gretchen Bellinger Inc., Cohoes, N.Y. (upholstery); Nancy Corzine, Los Angeles (upholstery); Scalamandre, New York City (upholstery); Mary Bright Originals, New York City (draperies); **Signage:** ASI Sign Systems, New York City; **Mannequins/Forms:** Major Display/Lorex, Terrebonne, Que.; Halper Smith, Quarryville, Pa.; **Stone Supplier:** American Stone Co., Houston

152 TIFFANY & CO.

THE WESTCHESTER, WHITE PLAINS, N.Y.

Design: Tiffany & Co. Store Planning & Design Department, New York City — Philip Bottega, AIA, vice president; Edward Sullivan, manager of construction; Mark Looper, AIA, store designer; Robin Buckwalter, director of visual merchandising; **Lighting Designer:** Martin Shaffer & Associates, Hoboken, N.J.; **Architect:** Levi, Sanchick & Associates, New York City; **General Contractor:** Planned Management Construction, New York City; **Fixturing:** Modern Woodcrafts, Inc., Farmington, Conn.; **Furniture:** Baker, Knapp & Tubbs, New York City; **Flooring:** Designweave, Los Angeles, (carpet); **Laminates:** Wilsonart, Temple, Texas **Lighting:** Reggiani USA, Inc., New Windsor, N.Y.; **Wall Coverings:** Tandem Contract, Inc., Monmoth Junction, N.J.; **Fabrics:** Lee Jofa, Inc., New York City (upholstery); Manuel Canovas, New York City (upholstery); **Signage:** ASI Sign Systems, New York City; **Mannequins/Forms:** Major Display/Lorex, Terrebonne, Que.; Halper Smith, Quarryville, Pa.; **Stone Supplier:** American Stone Co., Houston